A Note to Parents and Teachers

DK READERS is a compelling programme for beginning readers, designed in conjunction with literacy experts, including Maureen Fernandes, B.Ed (Hons). Maureen has spent many years teaching literacy, both in the classroom and as a consultant in schools.

Beautiful illustrations and superb full-colour photographs combine with engaging, easy-to-read stories to offer a fresh approach to each subject in the series.

Each DK READER is guaranteed to capture a child's interest while developing his or her reading skills, general knowledge and love of reading.

The five levels of DK READERS are aimed at different reading abilities, enabling you to choose the books that are exactly right for your child:

Pre-level 1: Learning to read

Level 1: Beginning to read

Level 2: Beginning to read alone

Level 3: Reading alone

Level 4: Proficient readers

The "normal" age at which a child begins to read can be anywhere from three to eight years old. Adult participation through the lower levels is very helpful for providing encouragement, discussing storylines and sounding out unfamiliar words.

No matter which level you select, you can be sure that you are helping your child learn to read, then read to learn!

LONDON, NEW YORK, MUNICH,
MELBOURNE AND DELHI

Created by Tall Tree Ltd
Editor Kate Simkins
Designer Jonathan Vipond

For Dorling Kindersley
Senior Editor Lindsay Kent
Senior Art Editor Rob Perry
Publishing Manager Simon Beecroft
Category Publisher Alex Allan
DTP Designer Hanna Ländin
Production Nick Seston

Reading Consultant
Maureen Fernandes

This edition published in 2014
First published in Great Britain in 2007 by
Dorling Kindersley Limited,
80 Strand, London WC2R 0RL
A Penguin Random House Company

001-277244-Sept/14

A CIP catalogue record for this book is available from the
British Library.

ISBN 978-1-40532-009-2

High resolution workflow by
Media Development and Printing Ltd, UK.
Printed and bound by L. Rex Printing Co. Ltd, China

marvel.com
© 2014 MARVEL

Discover more at
www.dk.com

Contents

DK READERS

PROFICIENT
4
READERS

MARVEL

FANTASTIC FOUR

Evil Adversaries

Written by Simon Beecroft

The Fantastic Four

The Fantastic Four is an amazing team of Super Heroes. The members of the team are the Thing, the Human Torch, Mr Fantastic and the Invisible Woman. They leap into battle against deadly villains who threaten Earth and its inhabitants. This powerful team fights aliens from outer space and human criminals who are too deadly for the army or police force to deal with.

The members of the Fantastic Four have special powers. The Thing has superhuman strength and power. The Human Torch can generate flames from his body and can even fly. Mr Fantastic can stretch his body to incredible lengths, while the Invisible Woman can make herself suddenly disappear.

Space mission
Reed Richards always dreamt of travelling into space. After university, he used his scientific abilities to build a space rocket. However, he underestimated the amount of protection the ship would need to shield it from dangerous cosmic rays.

Originally, the team were ordinary people. Mr Fantastic is Reed Richards and the Invisible Woman is his wife, Susan Storm. The Human Torch is Susan's brother Johnny, and the Thing is Ben Grimm.

Old friends
Reed Richards and Ben Grimm met at university and became best friends. Ben trained as a pilot and piloted Reed's space rocket on the test flight that changed their lives forever.

The Fantastic Four are (from left to right) the Thing, the Human Torch, Mr Fantastic and the Invisible Woman.

Super-powers

The Fantastic Four (the FF for short) got their super-powers after being exposed to cosmic rays during a flight into space.

Mr Fantastic is the leader of the group. He can bend, expand, stretch or contract his body. He can also flatten his entire body to the thickness of a sheet of paper. No bullet or shell can harm him.

The Invisible Woman can make herself disappear and can also make others disappear. She uses her mind to create powerful invisible force fields that protect her and others from harm.

Super suits
The FF wear blue costumes with a Fantastic Four logo. The Thing thinks the suits are for kids and often refuses to wear his.

The Human Torch has
the power to turn himself
into a super-hot fireball.
He can produce
red-hot flames from
anywhere on
his body without
harming himself.

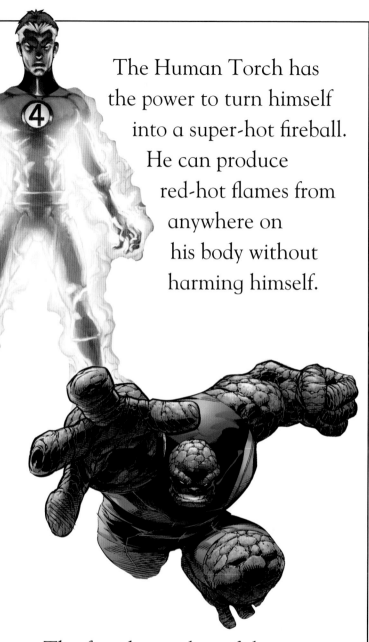

The fourth member of the team is
the Thing. He has superhuman
strength, and his skin is made of
thick orange scales, like armour.
Missiles bounce off his powerful body.

Ben is back
After Ben was
exposed to
the cosmic rays,
his appearance
changed and
his skin became
like rock.
He sometimes
returns to
normal, only
to turn back
into the Thing.

Crime fighters

The Fantastic Four live in New York City, but they travel all over the world and the Universe fighting crime. They have several different headquarters, including a tall office block called the Baxter Building.

The Fantastic Four's crime-fighting business is paid for by Reed's scientific research. He has given away many of his inventions to help people, but some of them he sells. Over the years, Reed has invented many incredible machines, including a hovering Fantasti-car and a flying jet-bike.

Fantasti-car
The Fantastic Four fly above the city in their amazing Fantasti-car. It has bulletproof windows and can separate into four vehicles for each team member to use separately.

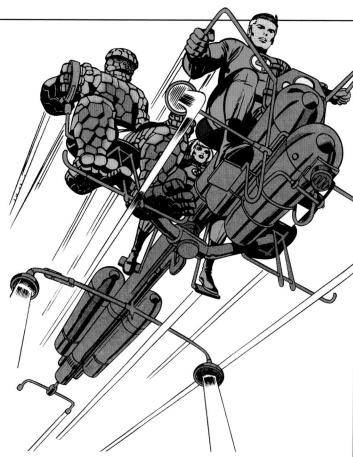

The team also has an airjet-cycle that is propelled by cushions of air.

Hi-tech HQ
The Fantastic Four use the top floors of the Baxter Building as their headquarters. After the original Baxter Building was destroyed, a new Baxter Building was built in space and teleported to Earth.

When the FF need to get together quickly, they shoot a special Fantastic Four flare into the sky above the city. The city mayor and the chief of police also have flare guns for calling the Fantastic Four in times of emergency.

Elder leader
The Mole Man
was originally
a scientist
named Harvey
Rupert Elder.
On a scientific
exploration,
he discovered an
underground
world. Elder
became the ruler
of the strange
creatures that
lived there and
named himself
the Mole Man.

The Mole Man

Soon after the Fantastic Four
formed, their first adventure began.
All over Earth, power stations
were mysteriously sinking into
the ground. At one power station,
a giant monster emerged from
the ground. The monster had been
sent to attack humankind by
its master – the evil Mole Man.

The Mole Man was
the ruler of a secret world
under the ground. Though
he was human, he hated
people. He sent his monsters
up to the surface to cause
chaos and destruction.

The Fantastic Four found
the entrance to the Mole
Man's underground kingdom.
A terrible three-headed beast
defended the entrance,
but Mr Fantastic made
a long lasso out of his arm.

He hooked the creature by its neck and dumped the monster in the sea!

The Mole Man set all his worst monsters on the fabulous foursome, but the Human Torch created a huge fireball that caused a rockfall. The monsters were trapped beneath the ground – along with the Mole Man.

Super senses
While Elder was exploring the world under the ground, he was blinded by a field of super-shiny diamonds. After that, he had to wear protective goggles. His sense of smell, touch and hearing, however, are incredibly powerful.

The Fantastic Four use their new powers for the first time against the army of monsters unleashed by the Mole Man.

11

Skrulls

Skrulls are ruthless aliens with green skin and pointed ears. They can change

shape into any person, animal or thing. Skrulls can disguise themselves as the inhabitants of a planet before they launch an attack on it.

Skrull leader
The Supreme Emperor or Empress is the ruler of all 30 billion Skrulls in the Universe. Many rulers remain in power only a short time before another Skrull assassinates them.

The Skrulls decided that the Fantastic Four were too powerful and must be stopped. Four Skrulls disguised themselves as the Fantastic Four and began causing chaos to turn the world against the superteam.

The police captured the real Fantastic Four and locked them up. After the FF escaped, they realised that they had to capture their doubles in order to clear their name.

Skrulls are a highly advanced race of warriors.

The FF forced the Skrulls to take them to their giant spaceship above the Earth. There, Mr Fantastic showed the Skrull leaders pictures of monsters in a comic book and told them the monsters were real. The Skrulls decided it was safer to leave Earth alone!

Turned bad
At first, Skrulls were peaceful aliens. Then, they made enemies of a violent race called the Kree. The Kree began attacking the Skrulls and slowly the Skrulls began to attack back. In time, they abandoned their peaceful ways and became aggressive.

The Super-Skrull

In an attempt to defeat the Fantastic Four, the Skrull Emperor created a supreme warrior called the Super-Skrull. This warrior had all the powers of the Fantastic Four. He could stretch like Mr Fantastic and burst into flames like the Human Torch. He had the strength of the Thing and could disappear like the Invisible Woman.

Chosen one
The Skrull Emperor chose the most powerful Skrull warrior to become the Super-Skrull. He put him through a harsh training programme and then altered his body so that he had the Fantastic Four's powers.

The Super-Skrull challenged the FF to a death-duel, but he was no match for the Super Heroes.

Mr Fantastic discovered that the Super-Skrull's amazing strength was coming partly from an energy beam sent to him through space. Mr Fantastic jammed the signal and defeated the Super-Skrull. He imprisoned him on a remote island in the middle of the ocean, far away from the energy beam's power.

When the Skrulls discovered what had happened, they projected an even stronger energy beam. The Super-Skrull escaped from his prison and battled the Fantastic Four, but the Super Hero team were too strong for him.

After two defeats, the Skrulls decided to punish the Super-Skrull by forbidding him to come home. The disgraced warrior wandered the Universe alone for years afterwards.

Secret power
Like all Skrulls, the Super-Skrull could change his shape. But his secret weapon was the ability to project a powerful hypnotic beam from his eyes.

Namor the Sub-Mariner

The Fantastic Four's encounter with Namor the Sub-Mariner began when Johnny went into hiding after an argument with the Thing.

In a cheap hotel, Johnny met an old, bearded man. The man turned out to be Namor, who had fallen on hard times.

Namor's powers
Namor the Sub-Mariner can breathe in water and on land. In water, he is one of the strongest creatures on the planet, but his power is weaker in the air.

Johnny dropped Namor back in the sea, where his powers were restored. Namor swam away in search of his kingdom but found it destroyed by humans. He was angry and swore revenge on humans.

Namor awakened a super-sized sea monster called Giganto. The mighty beast made its way towards New York City. No human weapons could stop it, so the Thing risked his life by entering the creature's belly with a nuclear bomb.

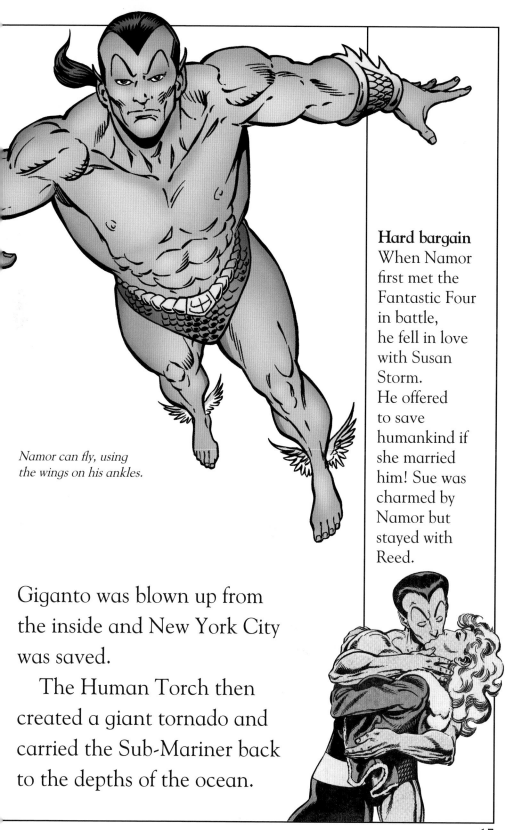

Namor can fly, using the wings on his ankles.

Hard bargain
When Namor first met the Fantastic Four in battle, he fell in love with Susan Storm. He offered to save humankind if she married him! Sue was charmed by Namor but stayed with Reed.

Giganto was blown up from the inside and New York City was saved.

The Human Torch then created a giant tornado and carried the Sub-Mariner back to the depths of the ocean.

Doctor Doom

The evil genius known as Doctor Doom devotes his life to destroying the Fantastic Four and becoming ruler of the world. He wears fearsome body armour and a metal mask to hide his horribly scarred face.

First meeting
Mr Fantastic and Doctor Doom went to college together. Victor Von Doom, as he was then known, was a brilliant science student. But he ignored Reed's advice about an experiment. The experiment went wrong, scarring Victor's face. He blamed Reed and has wanted revenge ever since.

A Doombot fires energy rays from its eyes at the Fantastic Four.

When Doom first appeared, he threw a giant web around the Fantastic Four's building. With Reed and his teammates trapped inside, Doctor Doom took the prisoners to his castle. There, he forced the Fantastic Four into a time machine. The villain ordered them to go back in time and steal the treasure of the pirate Blackbeard.

When the costumed foursome returned, they tricked Doom by filling the treasure chest with heavy chains instead of treasure. Doom was enraged and tried to kill the Fantastic Four. The team members had to use all their super-powers to stop him. But they could not stop the masked fiend from escaping.

Robot troops
Doom is highly talented at making robots and creates robotic copies of himself called Doombots. Sometimes, he sends the Doombots into battle instead of going himself.

Doom's scarred face is hidden behind a mask.

After his parents died, Victor was brought up by his father's friends.

Talent for evil
Doctor Doom is a master of science. He has built many weapons, including energy blasters and hypnotism guns. He can fly using a jet pack.

The origins of Doctor Doom

Victor Von Doom's story began in a small country in Eastern Europe called Latveria. Victor's father was a magical healer and his mother was thought to be a witch. They both died when Victor was young. Doom blamed the world for their deaths and swore revenge.

After the accident that left his face scarred, Victor was expelled from university. He travelled to the mysterious mountains of Tibet in Asia, where he studied the secret arts of sorcery with an order of monks.

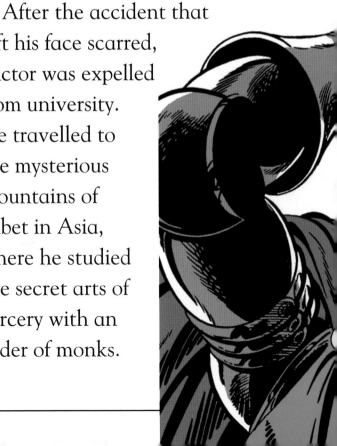

Victor forced the monks to create a metal mask to hide his scarred face. In his impatience, he put on the mask while it was still red hot, causing more scars. At that moment, Victor became Doctor Doom. He returned to Latveria and crowned himself ruler. His reign of evil had just begun….

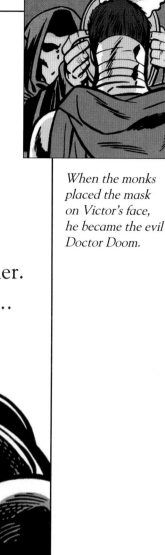

When the monks placed the mask on Victor's face, he became the evil Doctor Doom.

Combat skills
Doom's armour is nuclear-powered and computer-assisted. It is equipped with blasters and energy rays.

Puppet Master

In New York City,
a man stood at the top
of a high bridge.
In a trance, he got
ready to step off the
edge. Meanwhile, in
another part of the
city, the Puppet Master

Puppet powers
The Puppet
Master can
control only one
person at a time.
His power
weakens as
his victim moves
farther away
from him.

bent over a model of the same
bridge. His fingers reached out to
push a small puppet figure of a man
off the bridge....

The Puppet Master has the power
to make life-like puppets of people
from special radioactive clay.
He uses these puppets to control
people. The man on the bridge was
just a test of his power. When the
Human Torch rescued the man,
the Puppet Master plotted revenge.

The Super Villain carved a puppet
of the Thing and turned him against
his Fantastic Four teammates.

Mr Fantastic freed the Thing by turning him back to Ben Grimm. Then, the Fantastic Four defeated the Puppet Master.

Double take
After capturing Sue Storm, the Puppet Master disguised his blind step-daughter Alicia Masters as Sue to trick the FF. Alicia, who is the Thing's girlfriend, thought her father was playing a prank.

The Puppet Master models his puppets from radioactive clay. He plans to take over the world.

23

The Hulk

The awesome Hulk is the most powerful creature on Earth. As he gets angrier, his strength grows.

Secret identity
The Hulk is really the scientist Dr Robert Bruce Banner. Banner received a huge dose of radiation when he was caught in a nuclear explosion. Now, whenever he gets angry, he becomes the Hulk.

The Fantastic Four first battled the Hulk at a missile base that was being sabotaged. The general in charge of the base suspected the Hulk. The Thing and the Hulk fought a tremendous battle. In fact, a foreign spy was causing the damage.

The Thing has battled the Hulk on more than one occasion. When the Hulk turned up in New York City, only the Thing stood between the Hulk and utter carnage!

When the Fantastic Four teamed up with another Super Hero team called the Avengers, they drove the Hulk into the sea, where he disappeared. But not for long!

Fists of fury
Hand grenades and artillery shells cannot damage the Hulk's powerful green skin. When the Hulk slams his fists together, he creates massive shock waves that send his enemies flying.

The Hulk can cause earthquakes by pounding the ground with his fists.

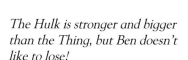

The Hulk is stronger and bigger than the Thing, but Ben doesn't like to lose!

25

The Mad Thinker

The criminal mastermind known as the Mad Thinker has no super-powers. Instead, he uses a huge network of computers to predict future events. This allows him to plan his crimes down to the smallest detail.

In an attempt to take over New York, the Mad Thinker tricked the Fantastic Four into leaving the city. Then, he took over the Baxter Building and helped himself to Mr Fantastic's secret weapons research.

When the Super Heroes returned, they had to defend themselves against their own weapons.

Big plans
The Mad Thinker plans to become the crime boss of New York City and then ruler of the whole country. Only the Fantastic Four stand in his way, which is why he needs to destroy them.

These included vibration guns and gas cylinders.

The superteam even faced a gigantic cyborg created by the Mad Thinker from Reed's own notes!

In the end, the Fantastic Four defeated the Mad Thinker because of the "x-factor" – the unexpected! The Thinker vowed to plan for the "x-factor" next time!

Robotic menace
The cyborg creature created by the Mad Thinker was nearly 5 metres (15 feet) tall. It had no face but could blast a high-powered tornado from its head. It could also turn into anything that it touched.

The Mad Thinker calls himself the Thinker. He believes himself to be smart not mad.

27

Rama-Tut

The Fantastic Four nearly met their match when they travelled back in time and met the evil Rama-Tut in ancient Egypt.

Rama-Tut was posing as a pharaoh, but really he was a time traveller from far in the future.

Time trouble
Rama-Tut, whose real name is Nathaniel Richards, comes from the 30th century. He was bored with the peaceful life there and wanted enemies to fight and monsters to defeat. One day, he came across a time machine built by one of his ancestors and left in search of adventure.

Rama-Tut's ancestor was Nathaniel Richards, Reed's father. Nathaniel left Earth after Reed's mother died and travelled to an alternative Earth.

Kang the
Conqueror

Scarlet
Centurion

Immortus

Rama-Tut used his ray gun to steal the fabulous foursome's super-powers. Under the influence of the ray gun, the Fantastic Four had no choice but to become Rama-Tut's slaves. Just when all seemed lost, the heat from the sun turned the Thing back into Ben Grimm. The ray gun no longer affected him, so he rescued his friends. Ben turned the gun on Rama-Tut, but the villain escaped in his time machine.

Other names
Rama-Tut travels to different universes. He takes different identities in each one. He calls himself Kang the Conqueror, Immortus and the Scarlet Centurion.

Diablo

Diablo is a master of the ancient science of alchemy. He uses potions made from herbs as his weapons. His potions can control a person's mind, lower their body temperature to freezing point, cause disturbing visions and much more.

Eternal villain
Esteban Diablo was born more than 1,000 years ago to wealthy Spanish parents. As a youth, he studied secret formulas and potions until he discovered a way to live forever.

The Thing actually started Diablo's diabolical career. Diablo had been imprisoned within the crypt of an abandoned castle for more than 100 years. The Thing set him loose while he was visiting the castle. Diablo created a potion to improve the Thing's appearance. Ben was so grateful to look more human that he agreed to serve Diablo for a year. Diablo built up an army to conquer the world. Just in time, the potion wore off, and Ben chased Diablo back to his crypt.

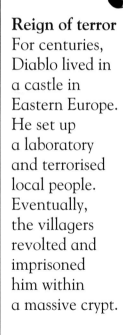

Reign of terror
For centuries, Diablo lived in a castle in Eastern Europe. He set up a laboratory and terrorised local people. Eventually, the villagers revolted and imprisoned him within a massive crypt.

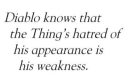

Diablo knows that the Thing's hatred of his appearance is his weakness.

Dragon Man

Strange creation
Professor Gregson Gilbert built Dragon Man in his university laboratory. Gilbert was a biologist specialising in super-powered humans. He never intended the robot to live, but Diablo had other plans!

The Fantastic Four thought they had seen the last of Diablo, but he managed to escape from captivity again. This time, he targeted a university professor who had created a robot dragon as a research project. Diablo used his potions to give the robot life. The creature became known as Dragon Man.

Dragon Man towers over human beings. He can breathe fire and fly using powerful wings. His tail is strong enough to swat the Thing away as if he were just a fly.

At Dead Man's Lake, a great battle took place between the Fantastic Four and Dragon Man. For a moment during the battle, Sue was able to make the creature respond to her kindness.

But Dragon Man was unstoppable as long as he was under Diablo's control. It was only when Diablo was distracted that Dragon Man turned on him. Both Diablo and the creature plunged deep into the lake. The costumed quartet had stopped yet another deadly plan.

Fearful foe
Dragon Man stands over 5 metres (15 feet) tall. His tail is powerful enough to shatter stone.

Dragon Man battles the Fantastic Four. It takes their combined powers to overcome him.

The Wizard
The Wizard wears a costume fitted with anti-gravity discs, which allow him to fly like the Human Torch.

Sandman
Sandman can transform any part of his body into sand and mould himself into any shape.

The Frightful Four

The evil genius the Wizard decided that four Super Villains were better than one. He put together a criminal double of the Fantastic Four. The three other deadly villains in the terrible team were Sandman, Paste Pot Pete (also known as the Trapster) and Madam Medusa. They called themselves the Frightful Four.

The gang stormed the Fantastic Four's building while Reed and Sue were holding a party to celebrate their engagement. They captured Reed, Sue, Ben and Alicia Masters. The Wizard put the captives to sleep and attached anti-gravity discs to each of them. These discs made them float into the air. The Wizard wanted them to float higher and higher into the sky until they would be unable to breathe.

Luckily, Alicia managed to send out a flare before she was captured.

Johnny saw it and came to the rescue. Quick as a flash, he "flamed on" and saved his friends.

Over the years, there have been many different members of the Frightful Four because the teams keep arguing.

The Trapster
Paste Pot Pete can fire sticky paste to trap victims and hold them for hours. The villain later changed his name to the Trapster.

Medusa
Medusa's super-strong hair is nearly 2 metres (6 feet) long. She can control every strand of it to attack people or even pick locks.

Galactus

Galactus is a creature with incredible destructive force. He travels across the Universe, surviving by destroying planets and feeding on their energy. Galactus wears a special suit of alien armour to contain his vast energies.

Galactus's base is a space station that is as big as an entire solar system.

Cosmic origins
Galactus was originally an astronaut called Galan. He was born on a world called Taa. When Galan learned that deadly radiation was destroying his planet, he decided to drive a starship into the heart of the radiation. Instead of dying in a blaze of glory, Galan was reborn as Galactus.

On several occasions, Galactus tried to destroy Earth. The first time, the Fantastic Four defeated him by threatening him with a device called the Ultimate Nullifier. This small machine was the only object that Galactus feared.

Nevertheless, Galactus always returned. Another time, it took the Fantastic Four and several other Super Heroes to defeat him. However, rather than watch the weakened planet-eater die of hunger, Mr Fantastic saved him.

Galactus can blast energy that is powerful enough to destroy a planet.

Silver Surfer
Some serve Galactus by seeking new worlds for him to devour. One of them was the Silver Surfer, who travels through space on a special surfboard. The Silver Surfer served Galactus for many years but eventually turned against his master.

Annihilus

Reed Richards fought one of the most crucial battles of his life against the powerful insect-like creature called Annihilus. When Reed's wife Sue was expecting a baby, Reed learnt that both Sue and the baby were in great danger. The cosmic rays that had given Sue her super-powers could kill both her and the baby. Reed had to travel to a weird realm of space called the Negative Zone to find a special energy that could save them.

Negative Zone
The Negative Zone is an alternative universe. Gateways connect our Universe to the Negative Zone. Reed found one of the gateways. He and the Fantastic Four have travelled to the Negative Zone on a number of occasions.

Annihilus is prepared to kill everyone who lives to protect his Cosmic Control Rod.

The energy was stored in a canister called the Cosmic Control Rod, but the Rod belonged to Annihilus. He guarded it fiercely because it gave him eternal life. Reed had to battle Annihilus until he could steal enough energy. Annihilus has hated Reed ever since and often tries to destroy him.

Great powers
Annihilus wears an armoured suit that prevents any injury and gives him the power of flight. The Cosmic Control Rod makes him immortal. It can also fire bolts of destructive energy.

Cosmic Control Rod

Overmind

The awesome Overmind has the mental and physical abilities of the entire population of a planet. An alien race called the Eternals created him. The Eternals were doomed to die so they chose their greatest warrior, Grom, and gave him the powers of their whole population. They sent him into space, where he continues their mission to conquer other planets.

When the Overmind first appeared on Earth, he used his hypnotic mind powers to stop people from noticing him. Only the Fantastic Four knew that he was plotting the destruction of the planet. The Overmind used his mind powers to make Mr Fantastic fight the Fantastic Four.

Mind power
The Overmind can blast his opponents with mind energy. He uses his mind power to force his enemies to do what he wants. He can also use mind power to move heavy objects.

The Overmind was too powerful for the Fantastic Four to defeat alone. In the end, a super-powerful being called the Stranger joined the battle. The Stranger had been hunting the Overmind across the Universe. He imprisoned the Overmind in a lifeless alternative universe.

Immortal being
The Overmind is unaffected by heat, cold, energy, electricity, radiation or disease. He is virtually immortal and does not age.

The Overmind can put thoughts into the minds of others. He is powerful enough to influence the Fantastic Four.

Terminus's
power comes
from his lance.
The mighty weapon
is 73 metres
(240 feet) long.

Terminus

The almost indestructible destroyer
Terminus towers over Mr Fantastic.
He attacks whole planets and
enslaves their inhabitants.
He carries a mighty energy lance.
This gigantic pole can create
atomic storms and steal
a planet's energy.

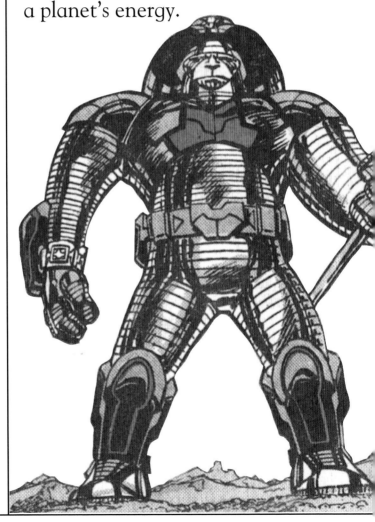

When Terminus first tried to invade Earth, Mr Fantastic was determined to stop him. Despite Terminus's great size, Mr Fantastic managed to knock the energy lance from his grasp. Then, he sent Terminus to the super-hot centre of the Earth. Terminus survived the fiery caverns, though it took him months to climb back to the surface.

Another time, Terminus returned to Earth and ventured down to the Mole Man's underground kingdom. Terminus took over the Moloids, one of the species of creatures that lived there. He wanted to use them to make himself a new body. To defeat him and rescue the Moloids, the Fantastic Four had to join forces with the Mole Man.

Metal casing
Terminus's mighty armour is made of living metal. If one of his body parts is injured or destroyed, he just grows another one!

Terrax

At first, Terrax was called Tyros. He was the ruthless ruler of a far-away planet. Tyros had the power to turn stone into living soldiers. The cosmic force called Galactus heard of Tyros's cruelty and gave him the power of superhuman strength – if Tyros would serve him.

Tyros became Terrax the Tamer. But he was too rebellious to serve anyone. He wanted to destroy Galactus and conquer the Universe for himself. So Terrax came to Earth. He used his super-powers to lift the entire city of New York into space. He told the Fantastic Four that if they wanted to save the city, they would have to attack Galactus. But Galactus returned New York back to Earth and stripped Terrax of his powers.

Terrible powers
Terrax's body is covered with a flexible rock-like shell that allows him to survive in space. A special form of energy also protects Terrax's body so he never has to eat or breathe.

Doctor Doom restored some of Terrax's super-powers, then sent Terrax back to New York to defeat the Fantastic Four. But Terrax turned on Doom. In the end, the Silver Surfer intervened. A terrific battle took place, and Terrax was defeated.

Magic axe
Galactus gave Terrax a magic axe that shoots out destructive energy waves. It can also project powerful force fields.

Terrax's power over stone is so great that he can move entire planets.

In one alternative reality, Reed was a child genius and was selected to work for a government research programme at the Baxter Building. Ben was at school with Reed and often protected him from bullies. At the Baxter Building, Reed met Johnny and Sue.

World's greatest!

The fight against vile villains and alien threats never ends for the Fantastic Four. Many of their adversaries appear again and again. The Fantastic Four also face many new enemies. One time, a female Skrull officer called Lyja disguised herself as Alicia Masters and infiltrated the team. In the end, she swapped sides and helped the FF.

The fabulous foursome also eliminated the threat of Devos, a giant armoured warrior. Then, they defeated a super-powerful force called Abraxas, whose cosmic power could destroy whole galaxies.

Reed and Ben were nearly buried in a military prison forever by Senso, a woman who could control people's minds.

Reed fought a deadly creature called Modulus who decided it was in love with Reed.

The Fantastic Four have fought many battles in alternative galaxies and dimensions, where friends and foes appear in different forms. Wherever or whatever the threat, the world's greatest superteam will always stand against evil.

Magician Doom
In his early battles with the Fantastic Four, Doctor Doom always chose science over magic. But then, he began to use his skills as a sorcerer more often. He wanted to fight Reed not with science but with magic.

Mr Fantastic, the Invisible Woman, the Human Torch and the Thing protect Earth and beyond from the forces of evil.

Glossary

alchemy
An early form of chemistry that sought to change ordinary metals into gold.

alternative universe
A universe that exists outside our own.

anti-gravity
A special means of making things float in the air.

artillery
Large guns or cannons.

assassinates
Murders someone, especially a ruler or other leader.

atomic
To do with atoms, the tiny particles of which things are made.

blaster
A kind of weapon that fires energy bolts instead of bullets or shells.

cosmic
Something that comes not from Earth but from outer space.

crypt
An underground cave, often beneath a church, that is used as a burial place.

cyborg
A living creature with robotic parts.

energy
Power obtained from various sources. Machines get energy from electricity.

expelled
Thrown out of school or university.

force field
An invisible barrier around an object.

galaxies
Vast groups of stars. Our sun is part of a galaxy.

immortal
Something or someone who will never die.

infiltrated
Passed undetected into enemy territory.

nuclear
Dangerous, destructive energy released when atoms are split.

pharaoh
The title of the kings and queens of ancient Egypt.

potions
Drinks with magical powers.

radiation
Rays of energy.

radioactive
Giving off energy.

sabotaged
Equipment deliberately damaged or destroyed by enemies.

shock waves
Destructive force caused by a massive collision or explosion.

sorcery
The use of magic.

species
A group of animals or plants. Human beings are a species.

superhuman
Powers that are far greater than those of ordinary people.

teleported
Moved by the power of thought alone.

tornado
A violent, swirling wind storm.

universe
All space and everything in it, including planets, stars and galaxies.